"Whether you're just starting your career search, were rece career change, this is a must read for you. Even if you're ha you take your career and life that one step further. Laura's book provided me the answer to the question I didn't know I needed answered."

Norm Creveling, President, Toyota Commercial Finance

"Laura Stone makes purpose come alive with a fresh recipe that serves up the ingredients for living purposefully. This is a 'must-give' book for parents, teachers, leaders, and anyone who is hungry to discover the power of their own purpose."

Richard Leider, bestselling author of *The Power of Purpose*,
Repacking Your Bags, & *Life Reimagined*

"*A Pocket Guide to Purpose* combines inspirational text and innocent illustrations akin to Saint-Exupery's *The Little Prince* — creating a simple and profound path toward the discovery of our purpose in life. A must read for those on such a search."

Jamil Mahuad, Former President of Ecuador
Fellow at the Program on Negotiation, Harvard Law School
Faculty in Executive Education Programs at the Harvard Kennedy School of Government

"To have every team member be fully engaged, leaders must understand their own purpose and the purpose of each other their people. This guide accelerates the process in an effective, dynamic, and unique way, making figuring out your purpose very accessible."

Sue Dodsworth, Chief Diversity Officer
and Vice President of Global Talent, Kimberly Clark

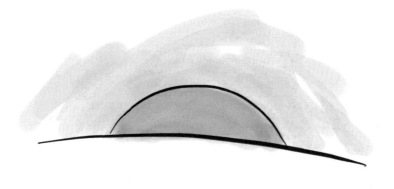

"A *Pocket Guide to Purpose* is a truly inspiring guide that will help anyone discover or remember their passion and true calling. It's powerful simplicity and playfulness make a very important topic accessible to all in just one sitting. I highly recommend this book to any leader, no matter how experienced or 'wise' they might be, as our journey of learning is a lifelong one."

Lynn Tetrault, Executive Vice President
Former Chief Human Resource Officer, AstraZeneca

"The beauty of this book is in its simplicity. It's straight forward, hopeful, inspirational, and playful. If you don't the have time or ability to attend a program in person, *The Pocket Guide to Purpose* is for you."

Scott A. Snook, Senior Lecturer of Business Administration
Harvard Business School

"A *Pocket Guide to Purpose* is a true, generous gift. Laura offers her core nuggets of wisdom, garnered from 25 years of work, that have hurtled me into deeply thinking about my life purpose in a refreshing, inspirational, and novel way. I am struck by the brevity and power of this pocket full of wisdom. A must read."

Amy Baltzell, Ed.D, Director of Sport Psychology, Boston University
Bestselling author of *Living in the Sweet Spot, Mindfulness & Performance*

"This book makes me happy! For anyone who has ever wondered how to dial up the joy in their life, A *Pocket Guide to Purpose* will put your hand directly on the pulse so you know exactly how to tune in and what to turn up in your life. Ultimately, you'll begin to see the path that you're meant to dance on through this precious life you've been given."

Haley Rushing, Chief Purposologist and co-Founder of The Purpose Institute

"I have done a lot of work over the years to get myself, teams I have been part of, and organizations, focused on purpose. I wish A *Pocket Guide to Purpose* had been available to help me with that work. The simple and compelling questions draw you in; each activity builds on the previous one, and before long you've worked through a thoughtful process to develop your unique purpose."

Michael Fischer, Vice President, Human Resources, Sysco

A POCKET GUIDE TO PURPOSE

A QUICK AND SIMPLE WAY TO ACCESS AND ADVANCE YOUR PURPOSE

LAURA J. STONE

ILLUSTRATED BY TAYLOR WRIGHT

Dear Stella –
May your purpose
emerge with Joy !
– Laura

No part of this publication may be reproduced, stored in a retrieval system, or transmitted in any form or by any means, electronic or mechanical, including photocopying, recording, and scanning, except as permitted under Section 107 or 108 of the 1976 United States Copyright Act, without the prior written permission of the author.
All rights reserved. Published in the United States by CreateSpace.
Name: Stone, Laura J., author and designer.
Classification: Self-Help / Motivational & Inspirational / Personal Growth / Happiness.
Cover design by Taylor Wright and CreateSpace.
Author's photo: Brady Holden, Holden Films.
Illustrations by Taylor Wright.
ISBN-13:978-1542694087
ISBN-10:1542694086
Library of Congress Control Number: 2017903769
CreateSpace Independent Publishing Platform, North Charleston, SC

TO MY CHILDREN, SOPHIE AND JACKSON.
YOU INSPIRE MY WHY . . . I LOVE YOU.

THE TWO MOST IMPORTANT DAYS IN YOUR LIFE . . .
~THE DAY THAT YOU ARE BORN
~THE DAY YOU FIND OUT WHY.

– MARK TWAIN

You are Invited....

TO TAKE A JOURNEY TO A VERY SPECIAL PLACE —
A PLACE TO EXPLORE YOU AND WHAT BRINGS YOU
JOY, ENERGY, AND PASSION. SO LET'S HAVE SOME
FUN, LIGHTEN UP A BIT, AND SEE WHAT SHOWS UP!
READY?

— LAURA J. STONE

THE PATH TO THIS GUIDE

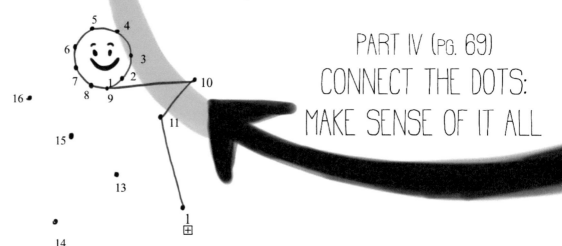

START AGAIN!

PART I (PG. 19)
AN OVERVIEW:
WHY THIS GUIDE

PART V (PG. 83)
KEEP GOING: PURPOSE IS
A LIFETIME JOURNEY TO
en *joy*

PART IV (PG. 69)
CONNECT THE DOTS:
MAKE SENSE OF IT ALL

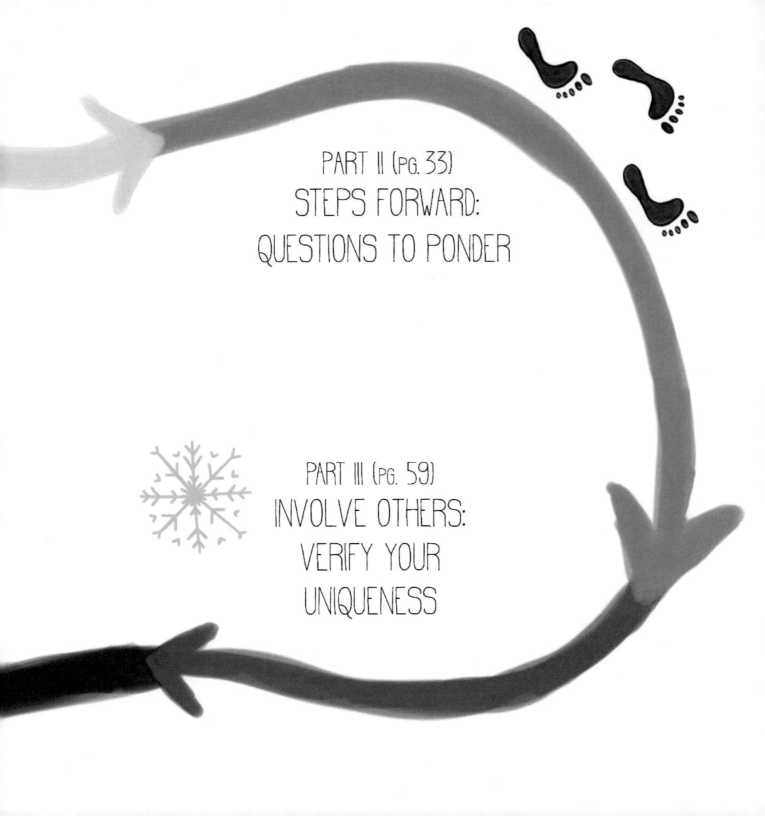

INTENTION AND INSPIRATION

My inspiration to write this guide stems from a conversation I had with a cab driver, Walter, in the fall of 2016. He was taking me to the airport in Dallas after an exhilarating and intense week working with corporate executives to help them identify and live their purpose. He asked what I was doing in Texas, and once I told him, his interest was piqued. I started asking him questions and a few short minutes into our conversation he exclaimed, "You are the answer to my prayers! I have been trying to figure out my purpose but didn't have the questions to get me going!" We arrived at the airport too quickly. I found myself wishing I had some kind of playbook I could hand over, something he could work with on his own, and left feeling frustrated that I had nothing to give him other than a tip.

The next morning I sketched out the story board for this guide. Over the next several weeks, I filled in the gaps, rearranged, added stick-figure drawings, wrote more, danced more, ate lots of dark chocolate, and sketched more. I knew the book had to be visual, simple, playful, and colorful — a physical manifestation of the joy that can be found in this process. While my ideas were clear, I eventually bumped up against the limits of my own artistic abilities. Thankfully, Taylor Wright, a gifted artist and my daughter's dear friend, brought my ideas to life with her wonderful illustrations.

Walter made me realize that I really wanted to help people press the "easy button" on the purpose process. I believe we all have gifts and interests, but sometimes we can forget what those are or de-prioritize them in service of our busy lives. Who has the time to wrangle through hundreds of books, scour the web, or spend thousands of days and dollars figuring this whole purpose thing out? Instead, this illustrated guide will give you a jumpstart by leveraging the same principles and ideas that have helped thousands of new and seasoned leaders I have worked with over the years.

I wrote this book for Walter, and for all of us who just want the essence — the gems, the nuggets to chew on. If you feel similarly, this book is for you.

My hope is that *A Pocket Guide to Purpose* will spark your imagination and be a catalyst to propel you forward toward a happier, more meaningful future. This process can be scary and exciting simultaneously. At times, you may think, "Am I really going to do this?" and at the same time say, "heck yeah!" because you know it is right for you. You are the only one who can do this work. Many of us go through life waiting — waiting for what should be to unfold before us. Finding purpose is a contact sport — it takes effort, intention, and choice. The good news is, if you're reading this, you're already making progress. Way to go!

But what is purpose, and why should you put in the effort in to find yours? The dictionary defines purpose as "the reason for which something is done or created or for which something exists." Why are you on this earth? What gifts do you have to share? Big questions — I know, questions that may seem difficult, maybe even impossible to answer. But what if you had the answers to these questions? How might that impact your life? There is significant and compelling research which suggests that having a sense of purpose is good for your mental, emotional, and physical health, well-being, and your overall feeling of satisfaction with your life. It increases resiliency and self-esteem, and decreases the chance of depression. The data is powerful and extensive. (For additional resources see p.113).

What I have personally experienced and witnessed with my clients, friends and colleagues is that having more clarity about your purpose has additional benefits. Purpose impacts how we make decisions, including the work we do (whether it is at home or in an office), how we do it, the people we spend time with, and how we spend our time with others. In essence, purpose can impact every part of our lives.

This book is not about inundating you with research, statistics, and graphs, or even extolling the virtues of purpose. Instead, these pages are intended to invite you to take a journey, to follow a simple process that will allow you to make progress in the purpose process quickly. Even the smallest steps can yield big rewards. Where has this journey brought me? After answering the same questions myself as those laid out in this guide, and receiving validation from dear friends and colleagues, I have realized that my Walter moment was no one-off. I love helping people figure out their purpose. I literally can't help myself from doing it, whether it's with the person stuck sitting next to me on a plane, or in a team meeting. I have also realized that my purpose lives in pictures. I came to understand that unlike some who think in paragraphs, I "see" process and purpose in a visual way. So the creation of this guide is a step in realizing my own purpose. THIS is the work I want to do. Now will it be this way forever? I don't know. But for right now I am on my way.

And it is with this in mind that I offer this guide. If it encourages you to take one small step, or inspires just one personal insight, consider it important progress in moving closer to understanding your purpose. We only have a short time on this planet, so why not spend it doing more of what brings you joy, energy, and meaning?

With the warmest wishes for your purpose to emerge in full color,

Laura

HOW TO READ THIS GUIDE

The sections of the book are laid out in five parts. Parts I and II help you ease into thinking about your purpose through a series of simple but important questions. Part III is where we add friends to the mix, to help you better understand yourself by how you impact others. We can't see ourselves from the outside. The perspectives of others reveal insights that are invaluable to the process. Part IV encourages you to step back and consider your answers to the questions and the feedback you received from others to see what patterns emerge. It is like making a collage or placing furniture in different spaces. You know when it clicks or when it feels right. Sometimes seeing things together in a new way can be very revealing. Lastly, Part V helps you think through the initial ways you might want to integrate your new-found purpose into your daily life. Even the smallest of decisions and actions can have wonderfully rich outcomes.

I encourage you to read this guide with a journal or pad of paper at hand, some vehicle for capturing your thoughts. It is important to write down what comes up for you as you answer questions and talk to friends. As fragmented a thought as you might have, as random an idea may seem, write it down. Going back over your notes a day, a week, or a year later can be extremely insightful, and is often where the most surprising set of patterns emerge.

This guide is not intended to be a one-time read. You will notice the that the table of contents is an oval, which represents a purpose journey that never ends. It evolves as our lives and circumstances change. Just when we come around the bend and think we may be finished, we have more paths to explore. We often find that another loop around shows us something we didn't see the first time, might even make us eager to continue to explore and take the path for a third time, noticing even more detail and wonder along the way. So consider reading through it once to get familiar with the territory (like taking a tour bus when you arrive in a new city to get the lay of the land). The second and subsequent times through, you may find yourself lingering on a page, an image, a quote. And when you do, grab your journal, call a friend, share with a coach, a parent, or a partner, and see where the pages take you.

I hope the information and questions will serve as a resource on an ongoing basis to ensure that you are living your most meaningful and empowered life. Most of all, enjoy the process! The journey is meant to be joyful and to aid you in getting one step closer to living your gifts more fully!

PART I

AN OVERVIEW: WHY THIS GUIDE

Why were you

PUT ON THIS ?

ARE YOU SPENDING YOUR PRECIOUS USING THESE ?

If not, why not?

MOST LIKELY BECAUSE YOU DIDN'T HAVE A

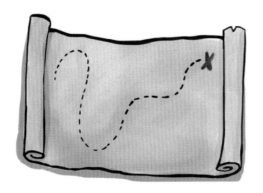

TO GET YOU THERE.

THIS WON'T TAKE

OR EVEN

2020, 2022 TO DO!

THIS WILL TAKE A LIFETIME BECAUSE WE CONTINUE TO EVOLVE AND OUR LIVES CHANGE.

IN MINUTES,
START A SIMPLE
BRING MORE

YOU CAN

JOURNEY THAT WILL

CLARITY

AND

FOCUS

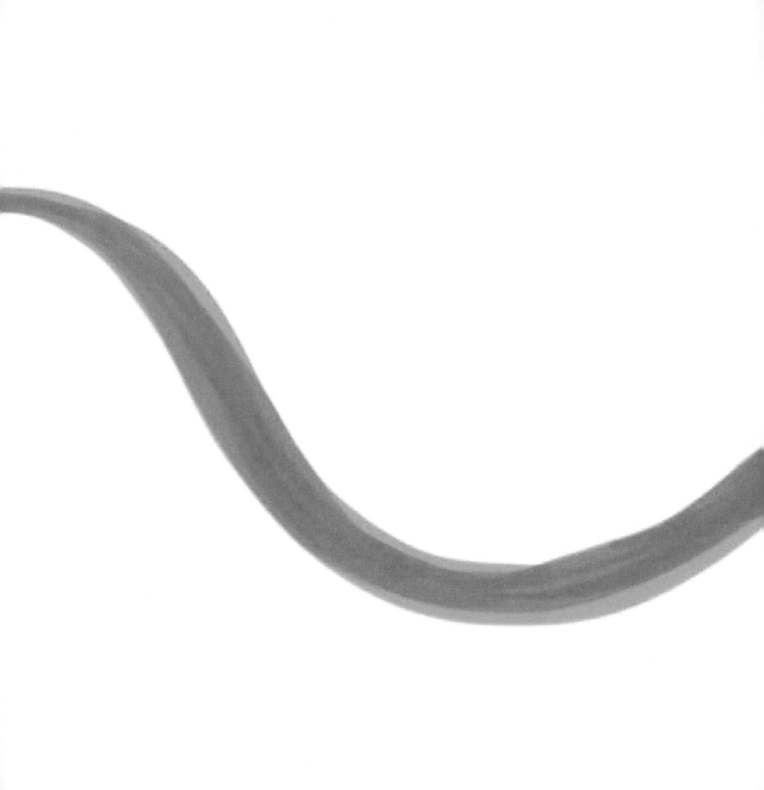

PART II

STEPS FORWARD:
QUESTIONS TO PONDER

BY THE TIME YOU ARE

AND ANSWERING SOME

BE CLOSER TO FIGURING

DONE READING THIS GUIDE

FUN ??? s, YOU WILL

OUT YOUR PURPOSE.

LET'S START WITH SOME ?S TO GET THE

GOING!

WHAT DO YOU ♥ TO DO THAT YOU'VE NEVER RECEIVED TRAINING FOR?

What can't you help yourself from doing that you've been doing all your life?

WHAT DO YOU DO THAT YOU LOSE TRACK OF DOING?

When do the hours  by ?

WHAT *big ideas* HAVE YOU BEEN DREAMING ABOUT THAT FILL YOUR SOUL?

DON'T WORRY IF AN IDEA DOESN'T COME RIGHT AWAY — MAYBE THE NEXT QUESTION WILL HELP REVEAL ANOTHER DIMENSION TO YOUR PURPOSE.

WHAT DO YOU WAKE UP THINKING ABOUT THAT MAKES YOU *excited* AND GIVES YOU *energy*?

WHAT DID YOU 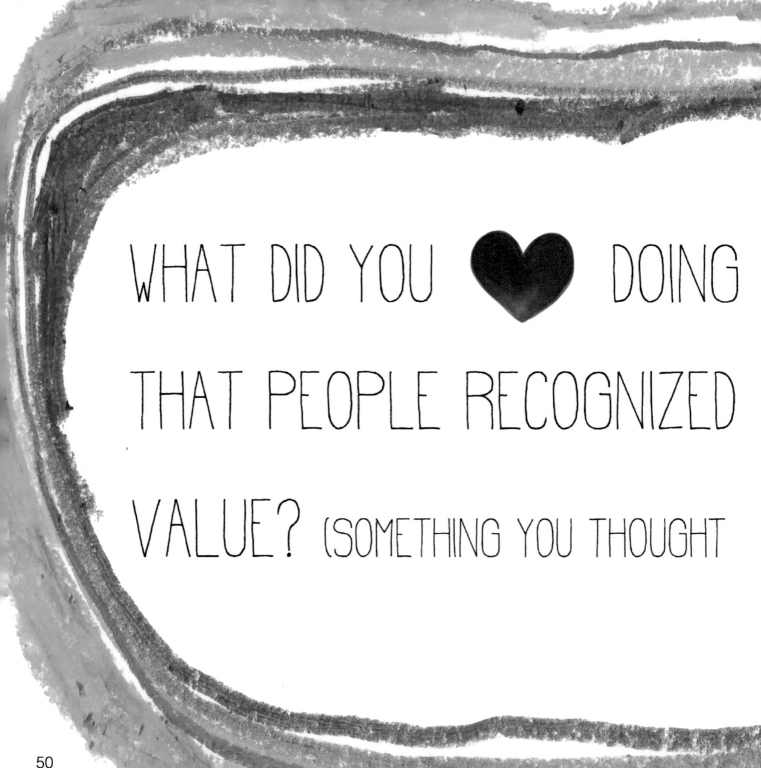 DOING THAT PEOPLE RECOGNIZED VALUE? (SOMETHING YOU THOUGHT

AS A KID (AND AS AN ADULT!)

IN YOU THAT YOU DIDN'T

EVERYONE COULD DO?)

NO, REALLY, THINK ABOUT IT— IT MAY POINT YOU
TOWARD THE THING YOU LOVE TO DO AND ARE GOOD AT.

IS THERE A HOBBY, OR AN
ACTIVITY SUCH AS

OR

THAT MADE YOU FEEL AT HOME, MADE
YOUR HEART HAPPY OR PUT YOU AT ?

WHAT ROLE DID YOU FRIENDS WHEN

WERE YOU THE RING LEADER? THE DREAMER? A PLAY DIRECTOR? TEACHER?

PLAY AMONG YOUR YOU WERE A KID?

ADVENTURER? INVESTIGATOR? CONFIDANT? THE ARTSY ONE? THE CHEF?. . .

WHAT ABOUT THIS ROLE OR HOBBY DID YOU ENJOY?

IT IS OK TO FLIP BACK.

WHICH QUESTIONS SPARKED SOMETHING INSIDE YOU? WHAT DID THEY REMIND YOU OF THAT YOU PERHAPS HAVEN'T THOUGHT OF IN A WHILE? WHAT DO YOU WANT TO REMEMBER?

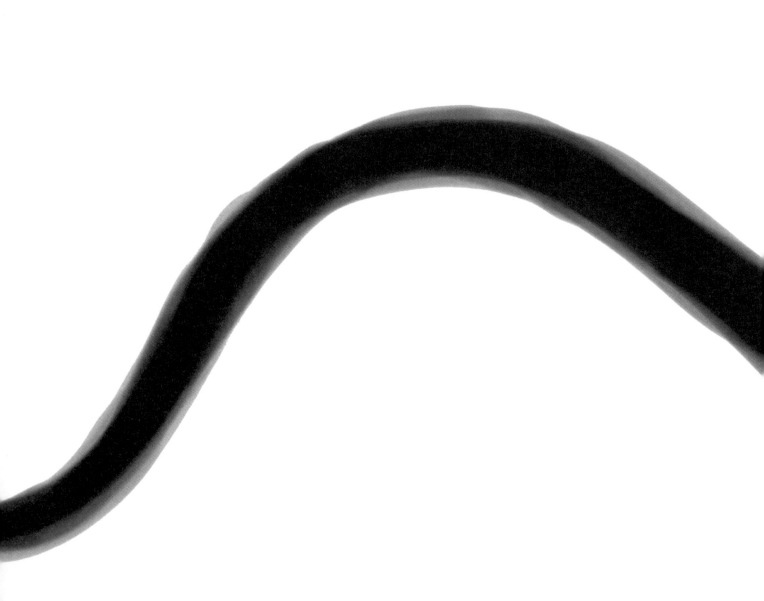

PART III

INVOLVE OTHERS:
VERIFY YOUR UNIQUENESS

WE ARE ALL

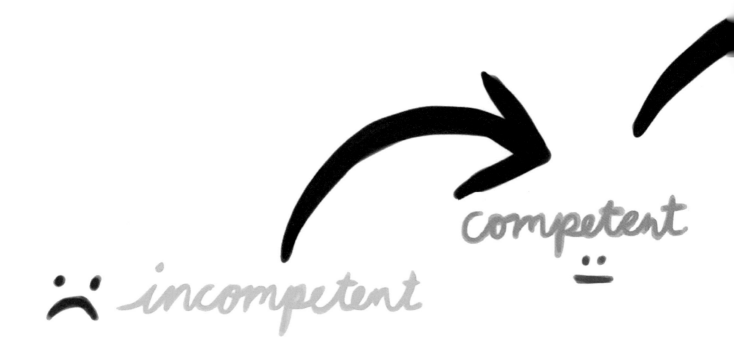

incompetent → competent

excellent

!!! Unique

AT SOMETHING.

SOMETIMES, NO MATTER HOW HARD WE TRY, WE ARE UNABLE TO SEE OUR OWN UNIQUE GIFTS. WE MAY TAKE THEM FOR GRANTED OR UNDERVALUE THE VERY THINGS THAT MAKE US SPECIAL.

SO HOW DO WE GO ABOUT IDENTIFYING THEM?

ASK!!!

FINDING YOUR PURPOSE IS A TEAM SPORT. WE ARE NOT MEANT TO DO THIS ALONE. WE NEED EACH OTHER.

ASK 10 PEOPLE WHO KNOW YOU . . . .

. . . FROM A RANGE OF PLACES IN YOUR LIFE — WORK, FAMILY, CHILDHOOD FRIENDSHIPS, ACTIVITIES, SCHOOL:

1. WHAT VALUE HAVE I BROUGHT TO YOU?

2. WHAT DO YOU THINK MAKES ME UNIQUE?

LISTEN CAREFULLY,

TAKE LOTS OF NOTES,

SEE WHAT THEMES APPEAR.

DON'T INTERRUPT AND TELL THEM THEY ARE WRONG. SIMPLY BE QUIET, LISTEN, AND TAKE LOTS OF NOTES, FOR YOU WILL FORGET THE AMAZING THINGS THEY ARE SAYING BECAUSE, AT TIMES, WE ALL FAIL TO REMEMBER THE GOOD THINGS ABOUT OURSELVES.

PART IV

CONNECT THE DOTS:
MAKE SENSE OF IT ALL

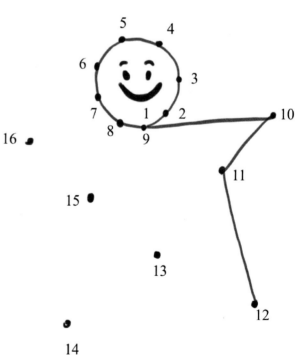

WHAT IS EMERGING?

WHAT PATTERNS CAN YOU NOW SEE?

HOW DO THEY CONNECT?

YOU ARE YOUR OWN SECRET SAUCE.

YOU ARE LIKE A KITCHEN FULL OF ALL THE PERFECT INGREDIENTS . . .

AND YOU HAVE ALL YOU NEED (FRIENDS, HOBBIES, HOPES, IDEAS) TO FIGURE THIS OUT.

AT THIS POINT, YOU MAY HAVE GENERATED SOME IMAGES, MEMORIES, INSPIRATIONS (AND MAYBE SOME PERSPIRATION AS WELL!) ALLOW THEM TO SIMMER, SET, THEN SEE WHAT YOU HAVE.

it's not science.

. . . IT JUST TAKES A LITTLE SPACE . . . (GET IT?)

YOU MAY WISH TO PAUSE HERE AND REFLECT. WERE YOU SURPRISED BY ANY OF THE ANSWERS?

DID ANY OF THE ANSWERS MAKE YOU FEEL UNCOMFORTABLE? MAKE YOU LAUGH? OR CRY?

PAY ATTENTION TO WHAT COMES UP FOR YOU WITH EACH NEW POINT OF VIEW ON THE WONDERFULNESS OF YOU!

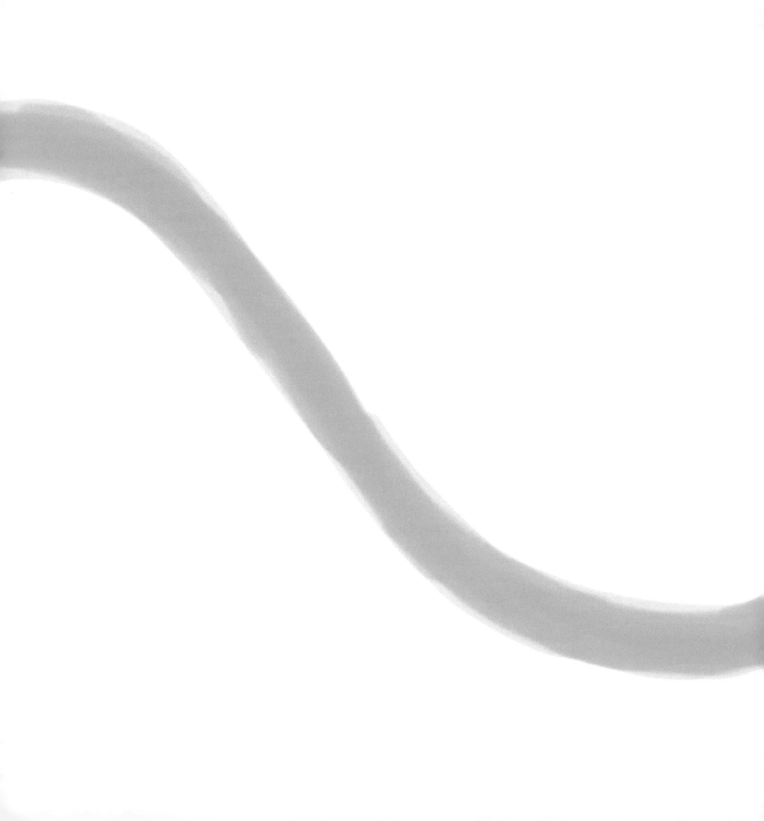

PART V

KEEP GOING: PURPOSE IS
A LIFETIME JOURNEY TO

enjoy

KEEP IN MIND

YOU DON'T LEARN ESPAÑOL IN A DAY.
FINDING AND REALIZING YOUR PURPOSE IS A
JOURNEY OF DISCOVERY.

And you already know it,

re·mem·ber (rəˈmembər) *v.* to come back to self

it's time to re·member it.

YOU MAY KNOW YOU ARE MAKING PROGRESS
WHEN YOU HIT ON SOMETHING THAT:

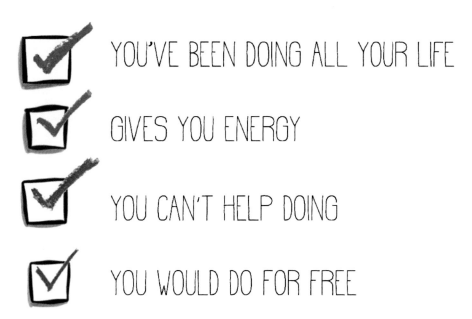

☑ YOU'VE BEEN DOING ALL YOUR LIFE

☑ GIVES YOU ENERGY

☑ YOU CAN'T HELP DOING

☑ YOU WOULD DO FOR FREE

ENJOY THE JOURNEY...

. . . FIGURING THIS OUT IS AN ADVENTURE!

LINGER . . . IT'S OK TO DAYDREAM HERE.

BLAST YOUR FAVORITE AND DANCE!

GO FOR A RUN TO PONDER THESE QUESTIONS . . .

SIT UNDER A TREE AND WATCH THE CLOUDS GO BY . . .

see what surfaces!

SO NOW WHAT?

EXPLORE WAYS AND PLACES TO LIVE YOUR PURPOSE EVERY DAY.

It is about

progress

not perfection!

MAYBE START SIMPLE . . .

WHAT SMALL CHANGE CAN YOU BRING INTO YOUR

EVERY DAY . . .

IN HOW YOU APPROACH YOUR DAY, HOW YOU
INTERACT, ASK QUESTIONS, LEAD MEETINGS?

EVEN IF TODAY YOU ARE NOT IN THE PERFECT PURPOSE-FILLED ROLE, PERHAPS YOU CAN FIND PEOPLE WHO ARE DOING MORE OF WHAT YOU WANT TO BE DOING — TAKE 'EM OUT FOR A Coffee

AND LEARN ABOUT THEIR

"TEST AND 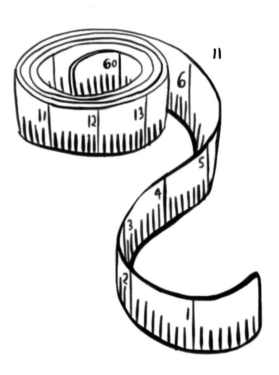"

DISCOVER RELATED

VOLUNTEER OPPORTUNITIES OR OTHER

JOBS IN YOUR COMPANY OR COMMUNITY.

THIS WAY YOU CAN QUICKLY

WHAT RESONATES FOR YOU AS WELL AS

MEET NEW PURPOSE PARTNERS

ALONG THE WAY!

THERE IS NO ONE RIGHT WAY TO FIGURE THIS OUT! EVEN THE EXPERTS DON'T HAVE ALL THE ANSWERS, ONLY YOU KNOW WHAT GETS YOU THERE!

LITTLE BY LITTLE . . .

 YOU WILL SEE MORE CLEARLY

HOW THE FIT TOGETHER.

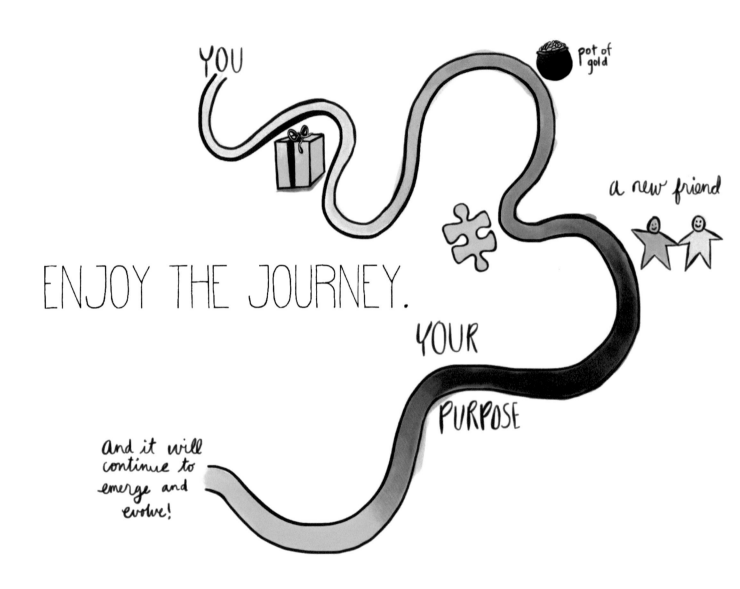

YOU

pot of gold

a new friend

ENJOY THE JOURNEY.

YOUR

PURPOSE

and it will continue to emerge and evolve!

AND BE KIND TO YOURSELF ALONG THE WAY . . .

MAYBE EAT AN  OR .

BOATLOAD OF GRATITUDE

To my family: My mom, Anne Evans — my biggest cheerleader — and my late father Sam, the quiet giant who always encouraged me to do what would make me happy. My children, Sophie and Jackson, who inspire me and whom I learn from every day, and to my husband, Lee, one of my best teachers. To my Pachamama Sisters: Thank you for all your feminine energy, inspiration, support, and love — Elizabeth Napolitano, Krista Anderson-Ross, Kathy Sherbrooke, Nancy Harrington, Michelle LaCharite, Sally Everett, Lisa Baffi, Lynn Tetrault, Mimi Welch, Janet Kraus, and Sherry Vogt. To my extended personal board of directors — you have helped me through some of my biggest transitions with great love, guidance, and wisdom: Tim Dorman, Kathy O'Neil Smith, John Haskell, Jack MacPhail, and Chad Rosen. To my early reviewers, cheerleaders, and colleagues: Madelyn Yucht, Susan Brady, Sarah Breigle, Rita Buscher, Guy McDonnell, Jon Magnuson, Stephanie Stamatos, Jamil Mahuad, Amy Baltzell, Dan Rattner, Russ Bankson, Norm Creveling, Scott Snook, Chuck Ritter, Sara Singer, Helena Foulkes, Sue Dodsworth, and Maisie Pollard. To my guides, truth tellers, healers, and ancient ones who helped me trust and honor my power, intuition, and my dyslexic gifts: Victoria Johnson, Emmanuel Illuminardi, Matt Hagan, Richard Whiteley, Crystal De la Cruz, Elizabeth Wilson, Diane Sanchez, Johan Harlaar, Normand Pellerin, and Brittany Stauffer. To my clients — I have learned something from each of you in the journey of making an impact in the world. To my childhood friends and roots who have a special place in my heart: Sammi Robertson, Margi Rosenthal, Stacey Creem, Lisa Nicklin, Julie Ketterer, Lani Wishnie, Ashley Barrett, and Sheryl Kalis. To the incredibly talented editors who set me straight in so many ways, especially in the final hours: Kathy Sherbrooke and Sarah Colwill-Brown. To the CreateSpace team: Thank you for guiding me so deftly through the publishing process — you all did GREAT work. And last but not least, to Taylor Wright, the gifted and talented illustrator who brought this book to life with such grace, creativity and brilliance — you are truly amazing.

Thank you!!!

JOYFUL MUSIC THAT BRINGS ME ENERGY, AND MAY HELP WITH YOUR PURPOSE EVOLUTION . . .

"Rumble and Sway," Jamie N. Commons

"Let It Grow" (Celebrate the World), Ester Dean

"Stronger," Kelly Clarkson

"Rather Be," Jess Glynne

"The Yellow Brick Road Song," Oleoka

"Light It Up," Major Lazer, Nyla, & Fuse

"Uptown Funk," Bruno Mars

"Happy," Pharrell Williams

"Trashin' the Camp," Phil Collins (sound track from Tarzan)

"Angels by the Winds," Sia

"Hey Mama," Matt Kearney

"On My Way," Phil Collins

"Can't Stop the Feeling," Justin Timberlake

"Lips Are Moving," Meghan Trainor

Anything by Kygo

"We All Fall Down," A-Trak, Jamie Lidell

What music brings you joy and energy? Maybe listen to some now!

WANT MORE RESOURCES?

Brown, Brené. Gifts of Imperfection: Let Go of Who You Think You're Supposed to Be and Embrace Who You Are. Hazelden, 2010.

Brown, Brené. Rising Strong: The Reckoning. The Rumble. The Revolution. Random House Publishing Group, 2015.

Burnett, Bill, & Evans, Dave. Designing Your Life: How to Build a Well-Lived, Joyful Life. Knopf, 2016.

Craig, N., George, B., & Snook, S. The Discover Your True North Field Book. New Jersey: Wiley, 2015.

Dweck, Carol. Mindset: The New Psychology of Success. Random House, 2006.

Frankl, Viktor E., Man's Search for Meaning. NY: Pocket Books, 1977.

George, B. with Sims, P. Discover Your True North. New Jersey: Wiley, 2015.

Hurst, Aaron. The Purpose Economy: How Your Desire For Impact, Personal Growth and Community is Changing the World. Elevate, 2014.

Ibarra, Herminia. Working Identity: Unconventional Strategies for Reinventing Your Career. Harvard Business School Press, 2001.

Leider, Richard. Calling Cards: Uncover Your Calling (deck of cards), Barrett-Koehler Publishers, 2015.

Leider, Richard. Power of Purpose: Find Meaning, Live Longer, Better. Barrett-Koehler Publishers, 2010.

Luna, Elle. The Crossroads of Should and Must: Find and Follow Your Passion. Workman Publishing, 2015.

Passion Profiler: www.thepurposelink.com/passion-profiler-tool.

Pink, Daniel. Drive: The Surprising Truth About What Motivates Us. Riverhead Hardcover, 2009.

Seligman, Martin. Flourish: A New Understanding of Happiness and Well-Being and How to Achieve Them. Nicholas Brealey Publishing, 2011.

Sinek, Simon. Start with Why: How Great Leaders Inspire Everyone to Take Action. Penguin, 2009.

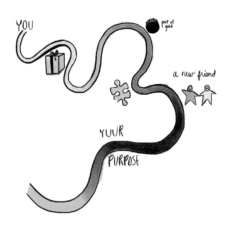

COMING SOON

My Pocket Guide to Purpose Journal

A Pocket Guide to Purpose for Teams

A Pocket Guide to Purpose App

Workshops

Webinars

Online Purpose Partners

10 Chairs: Perspectives from Many Seats

My Journey Map; Illustrated map to go along with *A Pocket Guide to Purpose*

… And other mysteries we don't even know yet!

ABOUT THE AUTHOR

Laura J. Stone is dedicated to helping others realize their potential and recognize their unique purpose. As a global leadership strategist, executive coach, speaker, facilitator, and consultant, she works with leadership teams and individuals, helping them to effectively and efficiently reach their goals. Stone has worked with major organizations and corporations, including Harvard Business School, GE, CVS, Fidelity Investments, and Unilever.

Stone received her bachelor's degree in English literature and French from the University of Wisconsin and the L'Institute D'American in Aix-en-Provence, France and studied energy medicine at The Four Winds. She is a former licensed 50-ton U.S. Coast Guard Captain and a former contributing editor to HRO Today.

Stone was included in the 2016 Women Worth Watching List by Profiles in Diversity Journal. She invites you to follow her on Twitter @stoneandco. Stone calls Brookline, Massachusetts, home. She enjoys spending time with her family and dogs, Bella and Pacha.

To contact Laura, you may reach her at Laura@pocketguidetopurpose.com. For inquiries, speaking and consulting engagements, please email: info@pocketguidetopurpose.com.

ABOUT THE ILLUSTRATOR

Taylor Wright attends Colgate University where she plans to study philosophy and educational studies and competes on the rowing team. Taylor calls Boston, Massachusetts home and lives with her family and her dog, Chip.

If you were inspired by something in this book, please share! We would love to hear about your stories, for they may help someone on this journey. Visit the website: www.pocketguidetopurpose.com.